A Dictionary of
Common Philosophical
Terms

Gregory Pence
University of Alabama
Birmingham

The McGraw-Hill Companies, Inc.
Primis Custom Publishing

*New York St. Louis San Francisco Auckland Bogotá
Caracas Lisbon London Madrid Mexico Milan Montreal
New Delhi Paris San Juan Singapore Sydney Tokyo Toronto*

A Dictionary of Common Philosophical Terms

Gregory Pence
University of Alabama -- Birmingham

McGraw-Hill

A Division of The McGraw·Hill Companies

**A DICTIONARY OF COMMON PHILOSOPHICAL
TERMS**

McGraw-Hill's Primis Custom Series consists of products that
are produced from camera-ready copy. Peer review, class
testing, and accuracy are primarily the responsibility of the
author(s).

3 4 5 6 7 8 9 0 QPD QPD 0 0

ISBN 0-07-242096-0

Printer/Binder: Quebecor Printing Dubuque.

A

ad infinitum: Latin, "to infinity"; without end.

a fortiori: Latin, meaning "even more so." If a particular argument is good enough to be accepted, then the same argument, strengthened, provides even more (a fortoriori) reason to accept it.

a posteriori: Latin, pertaining to truths which can be known only after observation and experience in the world. Contrasted with a priori.

a priori: Latin, pertaining to truths which can be known without prior observation or experience; a form of knowledge that humans may possess that is given to them without experience because it is innate or "hard-wired" in them. The truths of logic and mathematics are claimed by some to be known a priori. Kant argued that some a priori concepts such as that of a thing or time must be presupposed to have an experience in the first place. Contrasted with **a posteriori.**

absolute: (1) with complete certainty, which is unqualified, non-contingent and not relative to anything else; (2) one ideal reality which is completely independent and unconditionally real.

absolutism: in political theory, pertaining to the unrestricted powers of the state; in ethics, the view that some moral rules are required without exception.

abstract idea: A thought that has eliminated individuating differences between objects and moved from individual cases to a more general, inclusive category, for example, redness, canine, etc. The phrase is associated with empiricists such as Berkeley and Hume who denied that there are such ideas, holding instead that particular ideas or images stand for such abstractions.

absurd: see reductio ad absurdum

accident: that which is no part of the essential nature of a thing. An accident may be added or subtracted to an object without changing its essence. The color of a person's eyes is an accident; having a mind is not.

accident, fallacy of: see fallacy of accident

act utilitarianism: see utilitarianism, act.

actuality: from Scholastic philosophy, the state of being in reality rather than being in potential.

ad hoc: Latin, "toward this," a statement that may itself have little independent justification, but when added to a theory, saves that theory from rejection; in other words, a temporary fix.

ad hominem: see fallacy of ad hominem

adverbial theory of sensations: theory which states that the object of one's sensory perception is not an actual object, but an act that is being performed, for example, when viewing an orange sunset, one is seeing "orange-ly;" thus all perception is active, not passive.

aesthetics (also, esthetics): branch of philosophy that studies concepts of art and beauty.

affirming the consequent, fallacy of: see fallacy of affirming the consequent.

agnostic: one who neither believes nor disbelieves in the existence of God; one for whom the existence of God is a real, continuing, open question. A doubter of God's existence, but not as strong as an

atheist, who believes that God does not exist.

agnosticism: the stance of **agnostics** (see above).

akrasia: ancient Greek, incontinence, weakness of will; a condition where one knows a thing is good, desires that thing, yet still does not embrace it.

alienation: in Marxism, the estrangement imposed by the capitalist between the worker and his/her product, self, community, and humanity; in Existentialism, a feeling that the self is never really connected to other selves or the material world.

altruism: a disinterested benevolence and unselfish concern for the welfare of others, with no other end in mind.

ambiguity (ambiguous terms): when a word, term or phrase has more than one meaning; also called **equivocation**.

amoral: devoid of morality; operating completely outside the realm of moral value.

amphiboly: a sentence whose grammatical structure opens it to more than one interpretation, for example, "He bought a ticket to see the cheap dog trick." Here, the ambiguity lies in whether the dog or the trick was cheap.

analogical predication: in **Thomism,** the view that **predicates** such as "good" and "benevolence" cannot have exactly the same meaning when applied to God as when applied to humans, but must instead be understood by analogy. For example, God's forgiveness is similar to that of human forgiveness, but also different and greater.

analogy: a statement asserting that two things have something in common, for example, "Democracy is like sailing a ship: it works best when all members do their part."

analysis: the act of reducing a concept to its simplest and most basic elements in order to understand it better.

analytic philosophy: a style of doing philosophy that emphasizes the analysis of concepts in order to clarify and solve philosophical problems. Prevalent in North America, Great Britain, Australia and New Zealand, it is typically contrasted with **continental philosophy** (from the continent of Europe).

analytic proposition: a statement that is true or false by virtue of the meaning of its key terms.

anarchism (anarchy): position which holds that governments and laws are unnecessary and that communities should flourish without the coercion of the state.

anecdotal evidence: evidence based not on scientific inquiry, but on a small sampling and hearsay.

antecedent: within a **conditional** statement (in other words, an "if---, then---, " statement) the antecedent is the preceding, "if" part.

anthropomorphism: the representation of nonhuman creatures, for example, animals, nature, God, as having human characteristics.

antimony: a **contradiction.** The existence of two incompatible statements, each of which, taken on its own, is reasonable.

appearance (versus reality): the world as known through ever-changing, subjective experience, as opposed to deeper, unchanging reality.

aretaic (ethics): from ancient Greek, *arete*, "virtue." It proposes that the basis of ethical evaluation should be on the basis of character rather than actions because good character is the most valuable thing a human can possess.

argument (as a form of reasoning): a line of reasoning containing **premises** that support a **conclusion**; philosophers use this term in a technical way that differs from ordinary usage. "That was a really good argument you just made," would be a compliment among philosophers, not a sign that you were a trouble-maker.

argument from analogy: a form of reasoning asserting that, given two generally similar things, if one of those things has a particular feature, the other may also contain that feature. Arguments from analogy are strong or weak depending on the degree of similarity between the two things compared.

argument from design: a line of reasoning that argues that the intricate and complex nature of the world could not have existed without a divine designer, God. At the very least, it claims, if the universe shows evidence of intelligent design, then the existence of some intelligent Designer can be inferred as its cause. Also called the **teleological argument** for God's existence.

argumentum ad . . . : a way of classifying traditional fallacies in reasoning.

argumentum ad baculum: "appeal to force;" a fallacy that uses fear of dire consequences, intimidation, pressure, etc. to force acceptance of a conclusion that would not otherwise be accepted on rational grounds. "Anyone who wants a raise here better agree that the Yankees are the best team of the century."

argumentum ad hominem: "appeal to the person;" a fallacy of reasoning that attempts to disprove an argument by irrelevantly attacking the person who presents it. Frequently committed in public debates.

argumentum ad ignoranciam: "appeal to ignorance;" a fallacy that argues for a conclusion because no evidence is given to the contrary.

argumentum ad misericordiam: "appeal to pity;" a fallacy which uses sympathy as a way to redirect attention from relevant evidence in order to gain support for a conclusion that would not otherwise be accepted.

argumentum ad populum: "appeal to the people;" a fallacy which exploits the prejudices and widely-held beliefs of the people to gain support for an argument.

argumentum ad verecundiam: "appeal to authority;" a fallacy that appeals to an unqualified authority who, although knowledgeable in other areas, is without expertise in the subject area of the argument.

artificial intelligence: an area of inquiry that investigates the nature of intelligence and attempts to simulate it in computers and machines; often called "AI."

assumption: a principle or proposition that is unargued, taken for granted, and that forms the beginning point of an argument. The line of reasoning in an argument flows from these basic assumptions.

atheism: the belief or position that God does not exist.

attribute: (noun) a quality or characteristic that describes or refers to something.

autonomy (autonomous): the freedom to act independently of any external rule or authority. In Kant's ethical theory, autonomy of action is a **necessary condition** for moral choice.

axiology: the general science or study of value.

B

becoming: refers to the ever-changing world of experience where all inanimate and living things are said to come into existence, exist, then pass away. In Plato's universe, it contrasts with the unchanging, eternal world.

begging the question: the fallacy of assuming something to be true rather than proving it to be true; an argument for a conclusion that simply assumes its truth, without any other premises or any other reasoning; to beg the "question" or conclusion is to assume the very thing you should be trying to prove. Also referred to as circular reasoning.

behaviorism: a psychological theory that proposes the scientific study of human behavior solely through the observation and measurement of external behaviors, thereby classifying internal mental processes -- such as introspection, the unconscious, and thought -- as unscientific because they are unmeasurable or unobservable by others.

behaviorism, metaphysical: a branch of materialism that holds that mental activity and the mind are merely another aspect of human behavior and have no existence apart from it.

behaviorism, methodological: a way of investigating in psychology that restricts the data used in analysis to observable and measurable human behavior, thus excluding mental activity as a proper area of study. Contrasts with **metaphysical behaviorism**.

being: all that is real and nothing that is unreal is contained in the domain known as "being." In Plato's theory, it is a perfect and unchanging world of Forms (ideal essences), after which the changing things of this world's appearances are patterned.

belief: the mental acceptance of a statement as true.

benevolence principle: the belief that the happiness and good of others is desirable and that such happiness should be spread as equally and as widely as possible among the beings affected.

Big Bang theory: a cosmological model of how the present, expanding universe began: by a huge explosion of highly concentrated matter that occurred between fifteen and twenty billion years ago.

bioethics: the branch of ethics that studies moral problems in medicine and biological technology, for example, issues about **euthanasia** and cloning humans.

bourgeoisie: (French) defined by Frederick Engels as the class of capitalists who own the means of societal production and employ wage labor.

burden of proof: in a two-sided argument, where argument A is appropriately assumed to be true, side B must prove it untrue by proving B in order to win. In American justice, the prosecution has the burden of proof, since the accused is always presumed innocent. One strategy in debate is to try to shift the burden of proof to the opposing side.

C

capitalism: an economic theory in which property, production of goods and services are privately owned and traded for the profit of the individual or corporation, usually in a market where value is determined by price.

Cartesian doubt (method of doubt): a process of establishing knowledge based on eliminating any belief that might be false. It is associated with Descartes and advocates suspending belief in any proposition that can be doubted or that has even the barest possibility of being untrue. After all false beliefs are discarded, one builds on the remaining true, indubitable beliefs.

Cartesian dualism (interactive dualism): a worldview associated with Descartes in which two independently-existing, ultimate kinds of stuff are assumed to exist. Referring to the mind/body problem, it holds that the mind, although a substance separate from the body nevertheless interacts with the body, a different substance. "Mind" here is defined very broadly to cover anything mental, including thought, perception, and human will. Descartes thought such interaction occurred in the brain's pineal gland.

Cartesianism: the name applied to the philosophy of Rene Descartes.

casuistry: a method of evaluating ethical problems situationally, by analyzing the circumstances of a case. Casuistry contrasts with applying rules or principles to a problem, and rejects the idea that such application of rules or principles yields real solutions. Practiced in Scholastic ethics, it has been revived in modern bioethics.

categorical imperative: as a moral principle formulated by Kant, it directs: "act only according to that maxim that you can at the same time will that it should become a universal law." More generally, it is a moral requirement which must be obeyed with no exception. Categorical imperatives contrast with **hypothetical imperatives**.

category mistake: closely associated with the work of Gilbert Ryle, an English philosopher of the mid 20th century, it occurs when a thing of one category is incorrectly presented as if it was in another, for example, "He wanted to know where he could see the spirit of America." In this sentence, it is a category mistake to assume that the spirit of America is the category of things that can be seen.

causal explanation: the explanation of an event in terms of the causes of that event.

causation: one of the main philosophical problems examined in the area of metaphysics. It is the relationship that exists between two events where, when one occurs, the other always follows, and where the first makes the latter occur.

ceteris paribus: Latin, "other things being equal." Assumed in a context where one is implying something and where one is also holding external causes or variables constant so as to not affect the direct line of what one is implying. "If each worker spends more this year, ceteris paribus, the economy will grow."

clear and distinct ideas: a phrase used by Rene Descartes to describe those ideas that are so clear and distinct, so self-evident, and so impossible to imagine as false, that we must accept them, even when employing **Cartesian doubt**. The redness of a bright, clean fire truck is an example of a clear idea; the unique design of a fire truck, as opposed to all other trucks, is an example of a distinct idea.

consequentialism: the view that the value of an act should be judged solely on the basis of that act's effects on other beings. This is in contrast to *aretaeic* ethics where the value of an act is determined by the character of an agent or deontological ethics, where the value is determined by the intentions and motives of the agent. If one drops the maximizing premise (the one that directs us to create the "greatest" good for the "greatest" number) of utilitarianism (the greatest good for the greatest number), one gets the more minimal theory of consequentialism.

cogito ergo sum: "I think, therefore I am." From Descartes' famous *Meditations,* it refers to his certain, indubitable knowledge of his own existence as a thinking, conscious being.

cognition: refers to the process of knowing, thinking, and being aware.

cognitive science: an interdisciplinary science composed of philosophers, psychologists, computer scientists, linguists, among others, who explore the nature of thought and its connections to the brain.

cognitive: having to do with all the elements involved in thought, knowledge and awareness; opposed to the emotional and feelings.

cognitivism: the view that evaluative expressions, for example, "What a beautiful day!" are meaningful statements. More commonly, the view in ethics that statements involving morality can be true or false.

coherence theory (of truth): the theory that a belief is true because it is a member of body of a consistent set of beliefs that all hold together and make sense, and hence, need not rest on one certain truth. Contrasts with the **correspondence** theory of truth and **foundationalism**.

common sense realism: see direct realism

communism: an economic theory in which property and production of goods and services are owned communally, thus avoiding the need for market exchange of goods by price.

communitarianism: ethical and political theory that rejects the emphasis in recent ethics on isolated individuals, their rights, and personal autonomy, replacing this emphasis with a view of people intertwined by loyalty and love for families, communities, and friends.

compatibilism (compatibilist): claims that determinism and free will can both be true. In other words, every event may have a cause and I am still free to make my own choices.

complex idea: a concept composed of two or more simple, irreducible ideas, for example, "lemon" is a complex idea derived from a combination of "yellow," "sour," "round," etc.

concept: a term used to express a general idea of which objects are individual instantiations; for example, Lassie, Snoopy, and Ole' Yeller are instantiations of the concept, canine.

conclusion: the terminating point of an argument. In a valid line of reasoning the conclusion should be supported by the premises.

conditional statement: any statement or proposition which takes the form, "if---, then---."

confirmation: the degree to which evidence, collected through rational investigation, supports the conclusion it is meant to support.

connotation: the primary, objective meaning of a word, as opposed to its **denotation**, the objects to which it applies.

conscience: the awareness which conscious beings have that their actions are either morally right or wrong.

consciousness: a basic concept in the philosophy of mind, it is the awareness of all one's internal mental states, and external experiences.

consequent: within a **conditional statement** the consequent is the "then" part of the statement. See also **antecedent**.

contiguity (law of): associated with Gottfried Leibniz; it holds that nature makes no discontinuous "leaps."

continental philosophy: contrasts with **analytic philosophy**, it represents a spectrum of philosophical approaches developed in continental Europe in the twentieth century and comprises various theories of **phenomenology, existentialism** and **desconstruction**.

contingent: (1) a truth which could also have been false if circumstances had been different; (2) the state of being dependent on something else for existence.

contradiction: two statements which are mutually exclusive so that if one is true, the other is necessarily false.

contraries: two statements where only one may be true, but both may be false, for example, "All Americans eat apple pie," and "No Americans eat apple pie," are contraries because only one of the statements can be true and it is possible that both are false.

converse: reversed in position; "P implies Q" is the converse of "Q implies P."

corporeal: having to do with the physical body.

correspondence (theory of truth): proposed by Aristotle, it states that a proposition is true it correctly refers to things in the world. Contrasts with the **coherence** theory of truth.

cosmogony: see **cosmos**.

cosmological argument (for the existence of God): the argument that uses facts of the known natural universe, i.e. motion, causation, and contingency to infer the existence of God as the initial cause of these phenomena.

cosmology: the study of the origin and the nature of the universe.

cosmos: ancient Greek "order;" it has come to mean the organized universe, especially as subject to laws and principles of some kind.

counterexample: an example used to refute a general claim or principle, for example, a pine tree is a counterexample of the claim that all trees shed their leaves in the fall.

counterfactual(s) (conditionals): a **conditional statement** which contains an untrue **antecedent**, for example, if humans had three eyes instead of two, then there would be fewer traffic accidents.

creation ex nihilo: Latin, "creation from nothing;" the proposition that the natural universe was brought into existence from absolutely nothing by an act of God.

creationism: the doctrine that all species were created by God in one instant; contrasts with the theory of **evolution**.

criterion (plural, criteria): a condition which must be met in order to qualify an item's inclusion in a category, for example, in the statement, "Mammals are fur-bearing animals who nurse their young," being a fur-bearing animal who nurses its young are the criteria for inclusion in the category, "mammal."

critical legal studies: a view that the law is best thought about by reference to what actually occurs in courts and among lawyers; the academic side of **legal realism**.

critical realism: any view that acknowledges that our knowledge of the real, objective nature of the world is mitigated by the mind, on which sensory experience is necessarily dependent.

critical thinking: the analysis, criticism, and evaluation of statements claimed to be true and of arguments claimed to be valid.

cultural relativism: the ethical theory that moral evaluation is rooted in and cannot be separated from the experience, beliefs and behaviors of a particular culture, and hence, that what is wrong in one culture may not be so in another.

Cyncism (Cynics): a school of ancient Greek philosophy most closely associated with Diogenes of Sinope that called for arriving at true happiness by renouncing all external desires, and extolling the self-sufficiency of the desire to be a good person. The Cynics held that by reducing all material wants to the barest minimum, one will not disappointed in life: if one expects nothing, one lacks nothing. The common meaning of "cynic" in English does not represent the views of the philosophical Cynics.

Cyrenaicism (Cyrenaics): a school of ancient Greek philosophy most closely associated with Aristippus of Cyrene, its doctrine maintained that the only good was the attainment of happiness, as defined by "pleasure" defined broadly.

D

dasein (German, "existence, being") a term made famous by the German philosopher, Martin Heidegger, referring to the relationship of a person to surrounding people and objects, and hence, a term with a broader meaning than "conscious."

data (singular, datum): Latin "the given," it is that which is put forth as evidence and which serve as the basis for a particular inquiry.

deconstruction: a way of doing philosophy or literary analysis associated with Jaques Derrida that denies that there can ever be a correct, true interpretation of an author's works; instead of a simple act of understanding the intended meaning by an author, there are always many interpretations possible, especially by paying attention to notes, cultural context, the author's life, and what's implied in the work.

de dicto: Latin, "of what is said;" understood in conjunction with **de re**; something may be true about the statement (**de dicto**) or properties of the thing the statement refers to (**de re**). "The cat has four paws" is a de re statement. "The word "cat" has three letters" is a de dicto statement.

de re: Latin, "of the thing" (see **de dicto**).

deductive reasoning: a kind of reasoning where a set of **premises** is set forth from which a conclusion is necessarily drawn. If all the premises of a deductive argument are **true**, and if the argument is **valid**, then the **conclusion** must be true. An argument that is valid with true premises is called **sound**.

defeasible: that which can be overturned by a stronger and better consideration; it means literally, capable of being defeated.

definiendum: in a definition, that which is to be defined.

definiens: in a definition the phrase or sentence which defines the **definiendum**.

deism: a doctrine which affirms the existence of a Divine Being who created the natural universe, but which denies any additional interaction between the deity and its creations. Often in deism, this Being is seen as impersonal, remote and without human-like qualities. Contrasts with **theism**.

deity: a god or God; a supernatural being.

denotation: the object or objects to which a specific term applies.

denying the antecedent (see fallacy of)

deontological ethics (deontology): contrasted with **consequentialism** and **aretaic ethics**, and closely associated with Kant, it holds that the rightness of an act is derived from its logical consistency and universalizability. Deontological ethics famously holds that the right thing is obligatory without regard for consequences.

design argument: (see argument from design)

determinism: the belief that each and every event has a cause and that if all **necessary** and **sufficient antecedents** for a particular event existed again, it would be impossible for that event not to occur. This concept is traditionally associated with the problem of **free will**. The position known as **hard determinism** maintains that all behavior is invariably and without exception determined by causal factors beyond the control and responsibility of any individual, so that, in effect, free will and moral choice do not exist. However, **soft determinism**, a form of **compatibilism**, maintains that while there is a cause for all action, certain choices can still be made freely as actions that stem from the character or will of the agent, thus preserving the notion of moral responsibility.

deterrence theory (of punishment): a theory that is **utilitarian** in origin, holding that harming a person for a wrong committed is justified only if it serves both to deter the offender from future transgressions and if it deters others tempted to commit the same crime from so doing. In this theory, if there is no deterrent value in punishment, it is unjustified. Contrasts with **retributive** theories of punishment.

dialectic: ancient Greek, "conversation" or "back and forth." It refers to the use of reason to reveal truth and knowledge in any area of inquiry. Socrates used conversational dialectic to elicit truth. (See **also dialectical method**.) Hegel, and later Marx, posited historical forces that alternated between certain extremes, resulting in a higher synthesis; this historical pendulum is also called dialectic.

dialectical materialism: a dominant theme in Marxism; it proposes that the economic forces of society are more important than social or cultural forces, and that societies in history develop as swings between extremes. Such back-and-forth movement eventually brings on a higher synthesis (in Marx's view, the communist society).

dialectical method: the question-and-answer method used by Socrates to arrive at knowledge by exposing truths already implicitly known and by challenging the contradictions and flawed reasoning of opposing viewpoints.

dialogue: the process between two people of asking questions and giving answers.

difference principle: developed by John Rawls, it posits, as a principle of justice in creating the structure of a society, that departures from the presumption of equality are just only if the distribution of benefits and costs makes a society's most unfortunate members better than they would be under equality. For example, giving extra education and powers to physicians is only if such extra education and powers are better for the poor and sick than life would be with equal powers and education.

dilemma: a problem where one is confronted with two choices, either of which lead to an unacceptable conclusion. The "horns" of a dilemma are the two choices (**antecedents**) with which one is confronted.

direct (common sense, naive) **realism**:   holds that objects in the physical world possess all the characteristics that ordinary people believe they do.

disjunction: in logic, an "either/or" statement that technically takes the form, "p or q."

disjunctive proposition: a sentence that offers an "either/or" proposition.

disjunctive syllogism: see **syllogism, disjunctive**.

disposition: a tendency to be a certain way under a specific set of circumstances.

dispositional properties: the properties of a thing that are potential and defined in terms of what would happen if a certain set of circumstances were to occur; for example, polar ice has the dispositional property of solubility if above-freezing temperatures were ever to occur, whether such temperatures ever occur or not.

dispositions, mental: according to Gilbert Ryle, the observable characteristics of a person by which the mind may be understood, for example, likes and dislikes, habits, temperament, etc.

distributive justice: that part of **justice** which concerns itself with the fair distribution of benefits and hardships within a society. In medicine, distributive justice covers both allocative ("who-gets-what-and-why") issues that affect all of society, as well as issues of rationing, which affect particular patients or classes of particular patients.

double aspect theory: the **metaphysical** principle that mind and matter are but two underlying aspects of one reality.

double effect (doctrine of): a view in **natural law** ethical theory often cited in medical ethics about abortion and euthanasia. It claims that one may perform actions that could kill but the acts are permissible only if the agent does not intend the killing. Giving increasing dosages of morphine may depress respiration and kill a terminal patient, but so long as the physician only intends to relief suffering and not to kill, the action is allowed. In its strictest form, this doctrine holds that if an action has two effects, one evil and one good, then the action is morally permitted if: (1) the action is good in itself or not evil, (2) the good follows as immediately from the action as the evil effect, (3) only the good effect was intended in the agent's mind, and (4) the reason for performing the action was as important as that for allowing the evil effect.

doubt (method of): see **Cartesian doubt**

dualism (mind-body): the most well-known example of dualism, it proposes that mind and body are separate and distinct kinds of stuff that can never be reduced to each other.

dualism (ontological): contrasts with **monism**, it is the **metaphysical** view that reality consists of two qualitatively different kinds of things that are irreducible to anything else.

dualistic interactionism: the metaphysical view that the non-physical mind and the physical brain interact and causally affect each other. Descartes postulated that such interactions occurred in the pineal gland of the brain.

dualistic parallelism: the metaphysical view that the non-physical mind and the physical brain have events along two simultaneous, non-interacting tracks that do not interact or influence each other.

duty: that which ought to be done, either legally or morally.

E

efficient cause: one of the four kinds of causes distinguished by Aristotle, it is the agent by which a certain result is produced, for example, the efficient cause of a book is its writer.

ego: the self; it is the seat of all conscious thought, the organizer of all subjective sensory experience, and the originator of voluntary action.

egoism, psychological: a view in ethics or psychology holding that all human behavior is motivated by self-interest; this theory makes a factual claim about human nature, whereas **ethical egoism** makes a claim about how humans *should* act, regardless of the truth of **psychological egoism**. The view arises in ethics because, if true, it renders altruistic theories impossible. Hence defenders of altruistic theories see a need to defeat it.

egoism, ethical: an ethical theory claiming that the pursuit of self-interest is morally correct and rational; often associated with the Russian-born, American philosopher, Ayn Rand it claims that ethics would be less hypocritical if everyone acknowledged the truth of its claims.

eidos: ancient Greek, "form," it is used by Plato to refer to the perfect and unchanging Ideals or Forms, of which the things in the world are but copies.

eliminative materialism: a metaphysical principle that holds that inquiry into concepts of the non-physical mind should be eliminated, because such psychological inquiries (and their resulting "explanations") are so infected with error as to make them useless.

emotivism: the view usually associated with **logical positivism** claiming that ethical statements are mere expressions of emotion and, as such, have no basis in truth or falsehood. So "Abortion is wrong" is neither true nor false, but merely means, "I have negative feelings about abortion." Its most famous champion is the American philosopher, Charles Stevenson.

empirical: that which can be proved or disproved by sensory experience.

empiricism: a view championed by Locke, Berkeley, and Hume, and later by many American and English modern philosophers, that contrasts with the Rationalism of Descartes, Liebniz, and Spinoza, and which emphasizes that all human knowledge arises from sensation and experience, not innate concepts.

entailment: strong connection based on logical form; the relationship between a set of premises and its conclusion, when the conclusion is the only logical inference one can validly make. X entails Y, if X cannot be true without Y being true.

enthymeme: (1) a missing premise in an argument; (2) more often, an argument that is valid but that is only valid if some un-stated premise is made explicit.

epicureanism: a view associated with the ancient philosopher Epicurus, it encourages the pursuit and enjoyment in moderation of broadly-defined pleasures, for example, friendship, peace, and the contemplation of beauty, and it decries striving for material pursuits. The modern term is used in ways that contradict the original meaning of Epicurus.

epiphenomenalism: a view about the mind that states that mental events, such as conscious thought, subjective experience, and emotions really do exist but not in any way independent of the brain and body; instead, they are merely the effects of the physical brain. More important, such mental states can have no causal effect on the natural world or the human body.

epistemology: ancient Greek, *episteme*, "knowledge," the branch of philosophy that studies the nature of knowledge, how it is acquired, and whether true knowledge if possible.

equivocal: a statement or phrase with more than one meaning; ambiguous.

eschatological verification: the term used by John Hick to refer to a method, where the existence of God and other tenets of Christianity could be verified after death or after Armageddon. "Eschatology" is the study of "the final days," hence postponed verification in the future.

esse: Latin "to be," it refers to the state or act of being.

esse est percipi: Latin, "to be is to be perceived," the fundamental principle of Berkeley's idealism which contends that reality is immaterial or spiritual because its perception is dependent on some minds or Mind.

essence: that primary element of a thing, without which it would cease to exist.

essence precedes existence: Sartre's phrase that holds that before a thing can come into existence, it must first exist in **essence** in the mind of a creator. The phrase assumes a creator for each thing.

esthetics: see **aesthetics**.

ethical egoism (see egoism, ethical)

ethical pluralism: see **moral pluralism**.

ethical relativism: the ethical theory that denies the existence of universal moral truths and proposes that right and wrong must be defined variously, based on differences in cultural norms and mores. What is morally right is "relative to" one's society and time in history, not absolute across time and cultures.

ethical theory: see **ethics.**

ethics: the branch of philosophy that investigates and creates theories about the nature of right and wrong, duty, obligation, freedom, virtue, and other issues where sentient beings can be harmed or helped. Sometimes contrasts with **morality**.

eudaimonia: ancient Greek, "happiness or well-being," almost always associated with the ethical views of Aristotle, which posit eudaimonia as the meaning and goal of life, defined as honorable happiness among others in a cultivated, proud society that pursues science and the arts.

euthanasia: ancient Greek, "good death or good dying;" bringing about the death of another with the intention of preventing suffering.

evaluative statements: statements that attribute value to, or express a value, about something, instead of proposing a statement of fact.

evidentialism: the view that belief in anything is wrong without evidence. This position is usually used in arguing against a belief in God.

evil (problem of): the view that a benevolent, omnipotent, omniscient God is incompatible with the existence of real evil in the world. For example, "God knew about the Holocaust and could have prevented it, but didn't, so he doesn't care about us." Solutions to the problem of evil involve weakening one of the four premises, for example, denying that the Holocaust was an example of real evil or denying that its existence proves that God does not care about humans. **Zoroastrianism** denies the omnipotence premise by asserting that God has only limited powers.

evolution: a biological theory developed by Darwin to explain how higher life forms developed from lower ones. It proposes that through a series of genetic accidents, and natural selection of more adaptive beings in times of competition for scarce resources, living things of the present have come into being through billions upon billions of acts of reproduction over millions of years.

ex nihilo nihil fit – Latin, "Out of nothing, comes nothing'" a phrase originated by the Scholastics in claming that the universe needs God as its cause because something cannot be created out of nothing.

excluded middle, law of: the principle in logic that states that an assertion can be only true or false, and that there are no cases in between; there are no half truths or things "partly false, partly true."

existence precedes essence: a central principle of existentialism that holds that the essence of any human being is completely determined by the free choices made by that already-existing person. It denies that God or anything else created a human nature that makes humans a certain way. For Existentialists, what we know as "human nature" is not something we inherit but is merely a generalization we make from millions of ways of acting that people have chosen and hence, could have chosen differently.

existential proposition: a statement that denies or asserts that something exists.

existentialism: a term for the branch of modern philosophy that explores an assortment of questions having to do with the individual's lack of an essential nature, the absolute freedom he or she has to create his or here essence, and the modern problems of meaninglessness, alienation, the absurdity of life, and the absence of a rational meaning in the universe, etc. See also "**existence precedes essence**.".

extension: the extension of a word is the scope of the objects it describes.

external world: that which exists around us and is perceived and acted upon by body and mind.

extrinsic: a property that an object possesses only because of its relationship with something else, for example, a movie that is number one at the box office has the extrinsic property of being a box-office champion. It only holds that property in relationship to weekly box-office sales, not because there is something inherently within the movie that makes it a box-office champion regardless of ticket sales, or any other factor. This term is contrasted with **intrinsic**.

F

facticity: a term associated with Sartre, it is the totality of conditions that exist for an individual and which are capable of being known to be true or false.

faculty: one of the powers of the mind, for example, intelligence, memory, perception, imagination, etc., that allows us to know, feel and act.

faith: the belief in the truth of a doctrine that may not be capable of being proven true by reason or evidence, and which may require suspension of rational judgement through an act of will.

fallacy: a mistake in reasoning which traditionally takes two forms: a **formal fallacy** is an error in the formal structure of a **valid argument**; an **informal fallacy** is any other flaw including vagueness of language, irrelevancies, ambiguities, etc.

fallacy of affirming the consequent (formal fallacy) an invalid argument that wrongly concludes if A then B, and B, so A, for example, it is a fallacy to state the following: if John is at bat, then he is a baseball player; John is a baseball player, so he is at bat.

fallacy of appeal to ignorance; see **argumentum ad ignoranciam**

fallacy of denying the antecedent (formal fallacy): an invalid line of reasoning that denies the truth of a **consequent** because the **antecedent** is shown to be false; for example, the reasoning, "If I am a lottery winner, then I am rich; I am not a lottery winner, therefore I am not rich," is not necessarily true, particularly if said by Bill Gates.

fallacy of begging the question; see **begging the question**

fallacy, genetic: denial of an argument by explaining the origins (genus) of a belief, rather than attacking the rational basis for supporting it; for example, arguing that penicillin couldn't possibly be effective because it's grown from moldy oranges.

fallacy of hasty generalization a fallacy that draws a general conclusion based on an insufficient number of samples or on the basis of atypical samples accidentally encountered.

fallacy of popular belief; see **argumentum ad populum**.

fallacy of relevance: the use of a premise in an argument that has no bearing on, or relation to, the conclusion of an argument; for example, "Abortion is wrong because it kills a person. Hitler was in favor of abortion. Therefore abortion should be banned by law."

fallacy of smokescreen: the use of a diversion to obscure the salient point of a line of reasoning.

false dichotomy: the assumptions that only two possible conclusions exist in an argument, when really there are more. Also called the either-or fallacy.

falsification, principle of: principle made famous by the logical positivists that says that if an assertion cannot be proven incorrect by empirical or logical means, it is meaningless. Strong falsification says it must be in fact capable of being proved incorrect, whereas weak falsification only requires this in principle.

family resemblance: the notion that objects may be related not just because they share a common essence, but because they share a constellation of loosely-related, overlapping resemblances, like the appearances of people in a large, extended family. This view of concepts explains how a word or concept can refer to a class of similar things without having a common essence.

fascism: a political system championing the supremacy of a powerful charismatic leader such as Adolph Hitler or Benito Mussolini and that claims that the demands of the superior nation or race take precedence over the freedoms of the individual.

fatalism: the doctrine that all events are pre-ordained to happen and that no human action can influence their occurrence. In fatalism, events happen outside of, and despite, the choices of humans.

feminism: a movement that, descriptively, studies the different ways that men and women experience the world politically, ethically, socially, and epistemologically, either because of their different natures or because of their different gender socializations. As a social-political orientation, it seeks to eliminate bias based on gender and to value women's achievements, experiences, and perspectives.

fideism: the view that rejects the use of reason in gaining knowledge of the nature of God and holds that religious belief can be based only on faith.

final cause: one of Aristotle's four causes, it is the end or goal towards which a thing is brought into being.

first cause argument: a classic argument for the existence of God that states that because all events in the natural world must have a cause, God must exist as the first initiator of these events. It assumes that a regress without end back into time is unacceptable.

folk psychology: the set of beliefs and practices of ordinary people which posit mental states such as ideas, wants, and desires as causes of human behavior; **eliminative materialism** rejects this view.

form: a term that contrasts with the matter of a thing; shape. In Aristotle's metaphysics, a thing's matter is shaped into a form by a teleological essence.

formal cause: one of Aristotle's four causes, it is the conceptual blueprint that gives a thing its form or essence.

formal fallacy: see **fallacy**

formal logic: see **logic**

formalism: in **aesthetics**, a view that a work of art's essential characteristics are the only basis for evaluating it.

forms (theory of): see *eidos*.

foundationalism: term for any **epistemological** view that an adequate theory of knowledge must have a very certain base or foundation; contrasts with **coherentism**.

four noble truths: a teaching attributed to Siddhartha upon whom the teachings of Buddhism are based: (1) existence consists of suffering; (2) cravings are the source of suffering and bind us to existence; (3) suffering can be overcome by eliminating cravings; and (4) suffering can be overcome by means of an 8-step path, resulting in enlightenment.

free will: the capacity of humans to make choices free of coercion or compulsion and to choose the important actions of their lives.

free will defense: an attempt to resolve the **problem of evil**. Evil is explained because a benevolent God endowed humanity with free will and the greatest exercise of free will is to overcome the greatest adversity and temptation. Unless there were terrible things happening to people, there could not be saints. In essence, this defense denies the premise that real evil exists because what appears to be evil is here for a reason, to test us for salvation, to allow for saints, and to spur growth in character through suffering. See **evil, problem of**.

freedom: the political ability to act in a personal and private sphere without interference by the State, so long as one's actions do not harm others.

functionalism: a way of thinking about the mind that proposes that mental states are real but cannot, or should not, be defined by assuming an non-physical mind, but instead by their functions, particularly with respect to the behaviors they cause and produce.

G

genetic fallacy: see **fallacy, genetic**

ghost in the machine: a derisive term used by Gilbert Ryle to refer to the common view that the mind is a spiritual substance, or soul-like; a view that Descartes held.

gnosticism: ancient Greek, "knowledge," a branch of many religions that teaches that there are two kinds of teaching: one, the simple, dramatic one for the masses, which is used to attract people to the religion, and second, the real, subtle, less-dramatic teaching that is revealed only to the inner elite. Gnosticism contrasts with orthodox (literally, "straight-thinking") religion and is found in Christianity, Islam, Judaism, and almost every major world religion today. The Druids in Great Britain also practiced gnosticism.

greatest happiness principle: a view central to Jeremy Bentham and utilitarianism, holding that moral action requires that the greatest good be attained for the greatest number of beings, regardless of who the individuals who receive that happiness.

H

hard determinism: see **determinism**.

hedonic: from ancient Greek, "hedone," pleasure; that which has a pleasurable quality.

hedonic calculus: a method of calculating happiness in actual units by measuring an action's intensity, duration, immediacy, and number of beings affected. The concept, associated with Jeremy Bentham and his **utilitarianism,** holds that happiness is measurable, such that "the greatest good" can actually be ascertained.

hedonism: the ethical theory that claims that the pursuit of one's own pleasure should be the aim of all action.

hedonistic paradox: the view that intentional actions done in the pursuit of personal happiness are less likely to produce real happiness than the unintended consequences of some disinterested concern for others. This paradox was originally described by Aristotle, who observed that people who set out to be happy often aren't, whereas people who aim for excellence in some area often are.

hermeneutic circle: the difficulty in interpretation that results when an object or element which is part of a whole cannot be understood without the context of the whole, yet the whole cannot be truly known without an understanding of the original object or element. Thus, one cannot be understood without the other.

heuristic: a rule of thumb or a method for approaching a problem which, although not always completely accurate, helps to approximate a solution to the problem.

historicism: the term for a wide range of views that claim that all action must be interpreted in light of its historical period; likewise, understanding a concept requires knowledge of its historical origins and development.

homunculus: plural, homunculi, Latin, "little man," a postulate that what explains how we experience the world is the existence of a little person inside our heads who "sees" the world through our eyes; subject to an **infinite regress** in explaining how he, in turn, sees. Similar to the **ghost in the machine** criticized by Ryle.

humanism: any view that emphasizes the importance of human dignity, welfare and values, especially in contrast to theological or supernatural views.

hypothesis: a supposition that is advanced so that its truth may be put to the test, either empirically or through rational argument.

hypothetical imperative: Unlike **categorical imperatives** in ethics, hypothetical imperatives (or commands) are ethical obligations arising from a particular goal or desire, for example, "If we want world peace, we should destroy all nuclear weapons."

hypothetical proposition (statement): see **conditional**

I

idealism: in its more extreme form, a metaphysical view holding that reality is basically mental and that sensations are not produced by anything material; in less extreme forms, any view that denies that there is a reality independent of the mind and mental states.

identity of indiscernibles: sometimes called Leibniz's Law, it states that if two things share all of the same properties, then they are the same. It is a way of specifying when too things are logically the same.

identity thesis: also called "physicalism," the view in the philosophy of the mind that mental events are identical to physical events in the brain.

immanence: the state of being inherent in or coming from within something.

imperative, categorical: see **categorical imperative**.

imperative, hypothetical: see **hypothetical imperative**.

implication: a logical relationship between two statements where the truth of the first statement ensures the truth of a second. For example, given the statement, "Jane is a woman," one can draw the implication that "Jane is a human being."

Inauthentic: see **mauvais foi**.

Incarnation: "in the flesh;" in Christianity, the belief that God was born of Mary, raised as her son, and, as the man Jesus, learned of his divine nature and later, after Crucifixion, became one again with the Father.

incommensurability: the inability to arrive at a single measure by which two different things can be objectively assessed and compared; in ethics and economics, an important question is whether all values share one thing that can be measured. The field of preference economics avoids this problem by measuring what people prefer, and hence, substitutes a process for an answer about commensurable content.

incompatibilism (incompatibilist): a view that claims that **determinism** and free will are incompatible and cannot exist together.

indeterminism: the view that some things, including human choice, are not caused or determined; associated with Jean-Paul Sartre and existentialism.

indexical: a kind of expression whose meaning is dependent on the context in which it is said and therefore may vary with context. Personal pronouns: "I," "you," "he," "she," and "it" are examples of indexicals.

indubitable: that which cannot be doubted. Descartes wanted to build his views on indubitable truths.

induction: the process of reasoning that infers a general statement from a class of specific instances; contrasted with **deduction**.

induction, problem of: sometimes called Hume's problem, it questions whether it is justifiable to infer a general statement from some samples of a population because we never know whether the samples we've take are representative or skewed. More accurately, even if we have representative samples, there is an assumption that nature is basically and continuously uniform, such that standard samples will reveal the same kinds of things over time. Hume pointed out that we can never be certain that nature is uniform in this way.

inference: the process of drawing conclusions from a set of existing facts.

inference to the best explanation: a line of reasoning that permits inferring the existence of unknown, unseen and immeasurable entities, if this inference is the best way of understanding known facts.

infinite regress: an objection to a solution because it posits a series of explanations, each dependent on a previous one, going back without end into time. This objection is commonly made, for example, by the atheist Bertrand Russell, of the **first cause** argument for God's existence.

infinite: unlimited, without bounds, endless.

informal fallacy: see **fallacy**

innate idea: a thought that is believed to be inborn, present within the mind, at birth.

instrumental value: worth that a thing has because it contributes to a further good, not because it has **intrinsic value** of its own.

instrumentalism: the view that scientific theories are not capable of being proven true or false, but are merely instrumental in furthering scientific knowledge; also, the view that such theories should only be seen as instruments in the pursuit of truth, not the grander view that they themselves reveal truth.

intension: the meaning of a thing, rather than the members of the class in which it falls. Contrasts with **extension**.

intentionality: the aspect of our consciousness that is directed to something outside itself; the "aboutness" of our conscious states; in other words, the subjects and objects that are conscious states are directed to.

interactionism: the view that the mind and body are two separate and independent things that can influence each other.

internalism: the view that we directly experience the natural world in conscious states that can never be proven to relate to the external world in any objective way.

intrinsic: the property which an object possesses because of its nature which is independent of its relations to other things and their properties; contrasts with **extrinsic**.

intrinsic value: the worth a thing has in and of itself, independent of its relationship to any further end.

introspection: the process of examining one's own mental states.

intuition: the direct awareness of fundamental truths without aid of sensation or reasoning

intuitionism: in **ethics**, the view associated with G. E. Moore that knowledge of ultimate good and morality is apprehended directly by some special **faculty** in us of moral sense; the idea that certain fundamental and necessarily truths about reality are known directly, without inference or reasoning.

invalid (argument): see **validity.**

ipso facto: Latin, "by the fact itself;" the very fact.

irreducible: see **reducible/irreducible.**

"is" of identity: the meaning of the word "is" when it expresses the sameness of two things. For example, as in the statement, "Six things is the same as three things plus three things."

"is" of predication: the meaning of the word "is" when it is used to confer a property upon something. For example, as in the statement, "Her hair is short."

isomorphic: a term used to describe two or more objects which have the same shape or form.

is/ought fallacy: see **naturalistic fallacy.**

is/ought gap: the view, originated by Hume, that evaluative conclusions cannot be validly derived from purely factual premises. Hume held that people incorrectly move from "is" statements to "ought" statements.

J

justice: commonly divided into **retributive** and **distributive**, the former deals with punishments that correct the imbalance to society caused by a crime; the latter concerns the fair allocation of benefits and burdens in society.

justification: reasons for doing, supporting, or believing something; what backs up a belief; the evidence for a position.

justified true belief: very strict conditions for proving that we really know something, stating that we can only know something if and only if it is true, we believe it to be true, and we can demonstrate sufficient evidence that it is true.

K

karma: a central idea of Hindu and Buddhist religions, it holds that our inner self is affected y our actions in this life in future, reincarnated lives.

knowledge: see **epistemology**

knowledge by acquaintance: what we know as first-hand knowledge; the knowledge we obtain through direct experience.

L

laissez faire: French, "hands off," a doctrine championing non-intervention by the government in the marketplace; the basic idea is that when the government meddles in economics, it is likely to do so in the wrong way at the wrong time and, in the long run, to create more harm than good.

law of non-contradiction: a fundamental principle of logic wherein a statement and its negation cannot both be true or false at the same time; for example, "Our zoo has a giraffe" and "It is false that our zoo has a giraffe."

law of excluded middle: see **excluded middle, law of**

leap of faith: phrase associated with Soren Kierkegaard, originally referring to the unquestioned acceptance of God's will, even when doing so results in immoral behavior; now more generally used to refer to belief in God, or the incarnation of God-as-Jesus, despite reason and evidence to the contrary.

legal realism: a view that the law is best understood by analyzing what actually occurs in courts, law offices, and legislatures rather than by studying theories, concepts, or principles about law.

liar's paradox: an ancient **paradox** where some grammatical sentences seem to assert both truth and falsity at the same time. An example is the statement, "This statement if false," which can only be true if it is false, and only false if it is true.

libertarian: in the metaphysical sense, one who seeks to protect the concept of free moral choice by denying **soft** and **hard determinism**, and who also believes that free will really exists in a way that is neither causally determined nor just a random event. In the political sense, one who believes in minimal government and who opposes governmental intrusions into personal life. Libertarians tend to oppose laws against possession of marijuana and prostitution, and also to oppose programs of taxation that redistribute money from the rich to the poor.

liberty: the freedom to perform those acts that one wants to do. For example, the ability to say what one wants in public, without fear of reprisals.

logic: the branch of philosophy that examines the correctness of rational **inference**, the ways we think, and the limitations of such inferences.

logical positivism: a view associated with a group of philosophers in the early 20th century called "the Vienna Circle", it tried to generalize the scientific method to philosophy and, as such, rejected many metaphysical statements as meaningless. Its central concept was the **verification principle**, which posited that unless a statement was either empirically verifiable, or an **analytic truth** (a truth derived by logic), it was meaningless. Later positivists softened this position to allow meaning to statements that were potentially but not actually verifiable.

logical possibility: an event or thing that, while it may not be likely in this world, cannot be ruled out as prevented by the law of non-contradiction. For example, while cylindrical cubes are logically impossible, it is logically possible that elephants could one day fly (perhaps by genetic modifications).

logically possible world: a way of imagining alternative possibilities to our existence and reality, regardless of whether it is physically possible to bring it about, with the only criterion being that it doesn't violate the law of non-contradiction. The basic use of this concept is in modal logic, a branch of logic whose fundamental concepts are necessity and possibility.

M

Machiavellian: political ruthlessness based on the views expressed in Niccolo Machiavelli's *The Prince*, which advocated rule of a society according to what works, not according to absolute moral rules.

Manichaeanism: a doctrine of the Persian Mani, it flourished between the 3rd and 5th centuries A. D. and was probably derived from the much earlier, **Zoroastrianism.** In it, life and history are contests between co-equal God and Satan; hence, God is not omnipotent. Manicheanism, like Zoroastrianism, is a theological explanation of why the world has so much evil. Denounced as a heresy by Augustine.

Marxism: originally, the views of Karl Marx, the founder of theoretical **communism**, which includes the view that society will develop beyond capitalism through a revolution by the **proletariat** to a state where private property is abolished. Marx originated the labor theory of value (the value of a product should be equal to the amount of labor that went into it), which is often not its market value. He also analyzed the way that workers in big factories can be alienated from their work and argued that capitalism immorally allows rich people to make money from investing money without laboring.

master morality: see **slave/master morality**.

materialism: the metaphysical view that reality is composed only of causally determined physical matter and nothing else; the view in Marxism that the economic structure of society, for example, the inequality under capitalism and its resulting unequal economic classes of workers and owners, determine more than any other factors how social and political life work.

material cause: one of Aristotle's four causes, it is the material used to bring about an end result.

matters of fact: a phrase associated with Hume, it refers to statements that are grounded in empirical observation or personal experience, providing knowledge of the world.

mauvaise foi: French, "bad faith," it is a term associated with Sartre and refers to one's unwillingness to take responsibility for the self one has created by one's decisions when faced with crucial choices in life. Instead, one blames uncontrollable circumstances such as genetics, bad luck, and one's family for what one is. A person who does this is called "inauthentic".

meliorism: Latin, melior, "better," it is the view that the world is capable of becoming increasingly better through human action, thus improving the human condition. In theology, it is the view that God wanted the world to be as good as possible for humanity, a view that may contradict the **free will defense**, which holds that an evil world may provide the best test for salvation.

mention/use: when a word is placed in a sentence for the purpose of discussing it, it is mentioned. For example, in the statement, "The word "chick" is not respectful of women," the word "chick" is mentioned. When a word is placed in a sentence to further the meaning of the statement, it is **used**. In the statement, "The chick will soon become a hen," the word "chick" is used.

Note: in philosophy, students should be careful to distinguish the mention of a word from the use of scare quotation marks to emphasize an odd or different meaning of a word. For example, "Money is 'God' for them." is not an example of mentioning a word, but of using quotation marks to mean something other than actually quoting some person.

meta: in philosophy, a term referring to analysis not on the ordinary level, but at a deeper level that views the adequacy or inadequacy of concepts at the ordinary level.

metaethics: the study of the precise meaning and structure of the concepts, sentences, and words found in ethical reasoning. Ethics is about right and wrong actions in our world; metaethics is about the concepts and theories we use to think about those actions and about whether those ideas are adequate and true.

metaphilosophy: the study of the nature of philosophy itself, including its objectives, the appropriate questions for philosophical inquiry, and philosophy's relationship with other disciplines.

metaphysics (metaphysical): the branch of philosophy that investigates questions concerning the nature of reality and that moves beyond scientific inquiry to exploring questions about self, God, free will, and the origins of the universe. Named after a book by Aristotle for the study of questions left over after the study of this world, "physica" or nature.

method of doubt: see **Cartesian doubt**

methodological behaviorism: see behaviorism, methodological

methodological holism: usually contrasted with **methodological individualism**, the view that, in analysis in the social sciences (politics, economics, sociology) some social groups or institutions are not reducible to individuals.

methodological individualism: the view that any theory in the social sciences about social groups or institutions must invariably be reduced to theories about individual human beings, so that the individual becomes the primary basis for inquiry; usually contrasted with **methodological holism.**

mind: that which is supposed to be the seat of human **consciousness**.

mind-body problem: a perennial issue in philosophy: does the mind truly exist in nature as a separate entity from the body and, if so, as what kind of stuff or thing? Also, how do mind and body affect each other, if at all?

mind/matter dualism: see **dualism**

modal logic: a branch of logic whose fundamental concepts are necessity and possibility.

modus podens: the type of inference which allows us to infer B, if A always **entails** B, and A is present. For example, if a man is always a human, and if Socrates is a man, then I can infer that Socrates is a human.

modus tollens: the type of inference that allows us to legitimately infer not A, if A entails B, and not B. For example, if a bachelor is an unmarried male, and if John is not an unmarried male, then I can infer that John is not a bachelor.

monad: the basic, **irreducible** element of nature in Gottfried Leibniz's metaphysics.

monism: usually contrasted with **dualism**, it is the metaphysical view that all of nature is composed of only one substance. **Idealists** believe that the one substance is the mind, **materialists**, believe it is matter.

monotheism: the belief that there is only one God.

morality: what in fact people believe to be right or wrong, or how they in fact act; sometimes contrasts with **ethics** (the study of how they *should* act).

moral pluralism: strictly-speaking, it is neither a philosophical term nor a theory of ethics but a common view about morality; it holds that there are a variety of irreducible views about morality, none of which are entirely true, and more importantly, it posits that humans will never agree about which theory of morality is true. As such, it encourages tolerance when discussing ethical issues instead of simplistic absolutism.

moral relativism: see **ethical relativism**

mutatis mutandis: Latin, "the necessary changes having been made," in ordinary terms, making the necessary substitutions or changes.

N

naive realism: see **direct realism**.

natural law: objective principles for social, legal and moral behavior that are derived from what is believed to be the rational, ordered character of the world.

naturalistic fallacy: a controversial claim, originated by Moore, that evaluative concepts cannot be analyzed in terms of factual (naturalistic) terms. Sometimes this claim is associated with jumping the **is-ought gap**.

necessary/sufficient conditions: a **necessary condition** is a condition that must be satisfied before a thing can be included in a class or category, but it is not the only condition that must be satisfied before such inclusion. For example, being an athlete is a necessary condition for inclusion in the class of Olympic medallists. A **sufficient condition** is a condition that, when met, ensures an item's inclusion in that class. For example, being an unmarried male is a sufficient condition for inclusion in the class of bachelors.

necessary truth: a statement that is correct by virtue of its definition. For example, "a widow is a woman whose husband has died."

necessity: the property of a statement whereby it must be true and impossible to be false because it depends on no other **contingency** for its truth. For example, the statement, "for every number there is always a greater number," possesses the property of necessity.

nihil es in intellectu quod non prius fuerit in sensu: Latin, "Nothing is in the intellect that was not previously in the senses;" a central claim of empiricism claiming that all knowledge arises from the senses and experience and hence, that no knowledge is innate.

nihilism: in ethics, believing that nothing has meaning or value; in politics, believing that governments should be destroyed to create a better future.

nominalism: the view that rejects **universals** and holds that only particular instances of things are real, and that the only thing a class of items really has in common is its name. For example, humanity does not exist in general but only as individual instances of humans who only have a name, "humanity," in common.

non-falsifiable belief: see falsification.

non sequitur: Latin, "does not follow;" term for a **conclusion** that is not logically supported by its **premises**.

noncognitivism: see **emotivism**

normative ethics: the area of ethics that seeks answers to questions about which acts should be advocated and which prohibited; the phrase contrasts with **metaethics**.

noumenon: (plural, noumena) that part of reality that is not revealed by direct sensory experience; the underlying stuff beneath or beyond phenomena" and hence, a term used in dualistic metaphysics.

noumenal world: term associated with Kant, it refers to the world as it really is, beyond human experience, rather than the world we can experience and obtain knowledge about.

nous: Greek, "mind."

numinous experience: a phrase associated with theologian Rudolf Otto; sacredness, accompanied by a feeling of holiness and **transcendence**.

O

object: used either to refer to anything, abstract or concrete; also, any actual physical thing

objective: the kind of viewpoint that is unbiased by individual prejudices, sensory and perceptual distortions, or misinterpretations; contrasts with **subjective**.

objectivism: in ethics the belief that moral values can be objectively true independent of individual, subjective feelings. Capitalized, the word is used by Ayn Rand in a very different sense to defend **ethical egoism**.

obligation: what is required by law or morality; one's duty.

Ockham's razor: also referred to as the principle of **parsimony**, it holds that explanations should be as simple and economical as possible and that no more assumptions should be applied to an explanation than those that are absolutely necessary.

occasionalism: the **dualistic** belief that although mind and body are distinct entities that appear to interact, they do not; God alone causes effects; events in the natural world merely serve as "occasions" for God to work and bring about synchrony between mind and body

omnipotence: unlimited power, usually attributed to God

omniscience: unlimited knowledge, usually attributed to God.

ontological argument: ancient Greek, "ontos," being; a famous argument for the existence of God offered by Anselm, that states: if God is a supreme being, nothing greater than which can be conceived, and if we can conceive of such a being, then God must exist, because a supreme being cannot exist only in the imagination; if it did there could be a greater being - - one which exists in reality. This would contradict the original premise that God is a being, nothing greater than which can be conceived.

ontology: ancient Greek, "ontos," being; the branch of metaphysics which studies, questions, analyzes and criticizes assumptions and theories about the nature of being and existence.

open question argument: originated by G. E. Moore who argued that good cannot be synonymous with any other property, for then the question would always be relevant as to whether the thing that satisfies the definition really good? For example, if one equates good with pleasure and one presents a pleasureful thing as good, the question remains, is that thing really good? Therefore good has still not been defined.

operational definition: the definition of a concept in terms of the operations used to verify it. For example, loudness may be operationally defined in measurement of decibels.

ordinary language philosophy: a form of philosophy that analyzes concepts by looking at the their usage in ordinary language, in contrast to their built-up, acquired usage in the history of philosophy.

original position: see **veil of ignorance**

P

panpsychism: the belief that the whole of the natural world is composed of certain ultimate units that are conscious and sentient.

paradigm: a standard, framework, model, or pattern for a concept, around which subsequent investigation is structured.

paradox: the problem that arises when an argument with seemingly incontrovertible premises leads to contradictory conclusions.   A famous example is one of **Zeno's paradoxes**:   if a runner must run from A to B, first he must reach the midpoint, M.   Before he can reach M, he must reach the midpoint between A to M, which is N, and before N, the midpoint between A and N, **ad infinitum.** Therefore the runner can never start or complete the journey. Paradoxes are usually generated by an ambiguous term or terms and are dissolved by carefully specifying the key meanings.

parallelism: see **occasionalism**

parsimony: see **Ockham's razor**

particulars: individual things, as opposed to aggregates, or **universals**

Pascal's wager: associated with Blaise Pascal who argued that even if all arguments for God's existence fail, it is still the more prudential bet to belief in God, because if God does exist we have eternity to gain, and if God does not, we have lost little by believing.

paternalism: from Latin, pater, "father;"   the belief that restrictions on freedoms of the individual are justified when the agency, individual, or institution acts as a benign parent; in medical ethics, it was a view that came under attack after the patients rights movements attacked the paternalism of physicians, especially of male physicians to female patients.

per se: Latin, "in and of itself;" intrinsically.

perception: a central area of inquiry in **epistemology**, it is the activity by which we, with input from the senses, become conscious of and interpret the world around us into meaningful information.

perfectionism: the ethical theory that the ideal of ethics is to make oneself as perfect as possible, to make society similarly perfect, and finally, to perfect humanity

person: a major area of inquiry in metaphysics and ethics, it is usually defined as a being who is sentient, self-consciousness, has the ability to communicate with others, and is a self-moving agent. In this minimal sense, dolphins and chimpanzees may be persons, but some humans may not be if they are in permanent comas arld lack **sentience**.

personal identity: that property which causes a single individual to have consciousness of his or her own identity over and through time, it enables one to differentiate herself from all others. The major candidates for grounding this kind of identity are memory and the continuity of a human body over time.

petitio principii: Latin, "begging the question;" **see begging the question**.

phenomenalism: the view that the reality of physical objects does not exist apart from its **perception** by a perceiver and therefore, the material world does not exist apart from the actual or potential perceptions of the mind.

phenomenology: a non-homogeneous, twentieth-century philosophical movement associated with but not limited to Husserl, it is, most simply, the analysis of consciousness, the nature of essences as perceived in consciousness, and the nature of human experience independent of cause and psychological explanation.

phenomenon: (plural, phenomena) ancient Greek, "appearance;" it is that which is manifested or shown through sensory experience; contrasted
with **noumenon**.

philosophy: Greek, "love of wisdom;" it is the study of the most abstract and general questions about the world, and how we think, experience and should behave.

physicalism: the form of **metaphysical monism** that maintains that all existence is physical and can be governed by laws of physics. See also **identity thesis**.

Platonism: term referring to Plato's view that abstract concepts and numbers have an independent existence as (what is variously translated as) Forms, Ideals, or Essences, while physical objects are mere imperfect copies or shadows of these Forms.

pluralism: the view in metaphysics that reality is irreducible to one or even two things, and that there are several essential substances. Contrasts
with **monism** and **dualism**. See also moral pluralism.

positivism: a very general term describing various beliefs holding that
the **scientific method** is the best means of obtaining knowledge.

post hoc, ergo propter hoc: Latin, "after this, therefore because of this;" it is a **fallacy** that argues because B happened after A, therefore A caused B. An example of this fallacy is the statement, "The midtown bus stopped at Fourth Street where Mary got on and John got off; therefore Mary caused John to leave the bus."

postmodernism: a modern movement in philosophy and the humanities that rejects the optimistic view that science and reason will improve humanity; it rejects the notion of sustained progress through reason and the scientific method.

pragmatism: a form of American philosophy associated with William James and Charles Pierce that holds the truth of an idea should be measured by its practical applications in the ordinary world.

predestination: the doctrine that all individuals have been predestined from birth for salvation or damnation regardless of their deeds in life.

predicate: a condition; a property or attribute that qualifies another thing.

premise: a proposition or statement, a number of which make up an argument, from which a conclusion is finally drawn.

prima facie: Latin, "at first inspection;" on the surface; on the first look; something assumed until something better comes along or until a strong enough reason arises to overturn it.

primary/secondary qualities: **primary qualities** assumed to be inherent in an object as opposed to the qualities the mind perceives an object to have through sensory experience; they are very fundamental, abstract ones, such as "taking up space" or "being conscious." **Secondary qualities** are what we normally call sensations: redness, heaviness, roughness, and so on, and can be due to the interaction of primary qualities with our sensory organs.

prime matter: the ultimate potential from which all things take form.

prime mover: in Aristotle's worldview, the cause of all development in the universe. For Aristotle, the prime mover is merely a logical postulate, an X as the first cause, and completely non-anthropomorphic. It also "moves" the world by "attracting" development towards it, not by initiating development at creation.

principle of sufficient reason: see **sufficient reason, principle of**.

prisoner's dilemma: an ethical dilemma where two paired individuals must choose between two options: one which will benefit only one and harm the other, and the other choice, which will benefit both to a lesser degree, but only if both individuals choose it' hence a dilemma of prudential choice in an extreme situation.

private language: a term associated with Wittgenstein, it is a language that can be known only to one person because its terms are defined by the individual's subjective experience.

privileged access: the unique, exclusive, and unerring access we have to the processes of our mind by means of **introspection**.

problem of evil: see **evil, problem of**.

problem of induction: see **induction, problem of**.

proletariat: in Marxism, it is the oppressed working class, as opposed to the class of property owners, the **bourgeoisie**.

proof: an **argument** with such irrefutable **premises** that it establishes a justified **conclusion**.

property: that which is true of a thing; an attribute or characteristic.

proposition: that which can be stated in a declarative sentence, and which is capable of truth or falsehood.

psychological egoism: see **egoism, psychological**.

Q

Q. E. D.: Latin abbreviation of *quod erat demonstratum*, "that which was to be proved;" it signals the conclusion of an **argument**.

qua: Latin, "as."

qualia: the qualities of a thing that can be experienced by the direct sensory perception of that thing, for example, the sweetness of a peach, the softness and fuzziness of its skin, are all qualia.

qualities: see **primary/secondary qualities**.

quietism: the theological concept that rejects active involvement in the world in favor of quiet contemplation and passivity.

R

rationalism: a view in epistemology claiming that reason is the primary source of knowledge and truth, not sensation; modern rationalists weaken this claim to assert merely that reason can give us some knowledge independent of the senses.

realism: the opposite of **idealism**, it is the belief that objects in the physical world have an existence independent of the mind.

reason: the faculty of the **mind** that has to do with logic, analysis and rationality.

reducible/irreducible: capable of being broken down into smaller parts and especially in philosophy, by analysis. Irreducible implies that no further breaking down or analysis is possible.

reductio ad absurdum: Latin, "reduction to absurdity," it is a strategy used to refute an argument by demonstrating that something absurd results from it, so that the premises or inference must be rejected.

reductionism: a program in science that attempts to explain complex things in more fundamental terms, for example, anatomy was once taught by understanding gross structure, then it progressed to understanding functions of the body at the cellular level, then to the biochemical level, and one day, it may be reduced to the level of physics. Each step is reductionistic. Some theorists oppose reductionism, saying too much is lost, for example, in explaining conscious states as the simple firing of neurons.

reflective equilibrium: In John Rawls' theory of justice, equilibrium or balance is obtained when our rock-bottom moral beliefs are weighted against the fundamental principles of justice (assuming some give-and-take must take place in real-world applications), resulting in this state.

reification: the act by which an abstract idea or concept is assumed to be a concrete reality, merely because it has verbal form; generally, this word is negative and connotes a mistake, as in, "He thought numbers were things he could catch."

relativism: see both **cultural relativism** and **ethical relativism**

representative ideas (perceptions), theory of: the view that knowledge of the external world through direct sensory experience only represents or copies the real features of objects in the external world. One problem with this view is that the redness of a fire truck may be more in the *interaction* of the matter of the truck with our eyes than "in" the truck itself.

res cogitans: Latin, "a thinking thing;" according to Descartes, one of two substances, (the other is **res extensa)** that are **irreducible** to anything else and entirely different from each other.

res extensa: Latin, "that which is extended;" according to Descartes, the physical world; matter, including the matter of people, their bodies; that which takes up space and is in space. For Descartes, quantifiable stuff subject to the laws of physics and mathematics.

retribution: punishment for a misdeed.

retributive justice: that part of the theory of justice which considers punishment on the basis of just desserts rather than on the basis of deterrence or rehabilitation, based on the idea of compensating for an injury; based on the idea of "an eye for an eye, a life for a life."

rights: that which one is due; there are legal rights, natural rights, human rights, and moral rights in a particular society. Rights are often short-hand for moral rules about how people should get along, for example, the right to a smoke-free workplace is becoming an ethical and legal right in contemporary American society.

rule-utilitarianism: see **utilitarianism, rule.**

S

scepticism: see **skepticism**

scholasticism: theological philosophy, based on Aristotle's teachings and the work of Church scholars, taught primarily in medieval times (11th to 16th centuries) in religious training institutions.

secondary qualities: see **primary/secondary qualities**

semantics: a branch of **semiotics**, it studies the meaning of words and the relationship between the symbols of language and the actual world, whereas **syntax** studies grammar and the relation between kinds of words.

semiotics: the general study of signs and symbols, including the study of language.

sensation: that which is experienced by means of one or more of the five senses, through direct contact with the natural world. Sensation usually excludes purely mental events such as thoughts and ideas which arise internally in consciousness.

sense data: the information provided to us by our senses.

sentience: the ability to feel pleasure and pain.

skepticism: from the Greek skepsis, "questioning," in its most general use, it refers to a disbelieving and questioning state of mind; as a philosophical principle, it rejects the notion that real knowledge or truth are possible, perhaps because the mind is incapable of finding truth.

slave/master morality: slave morality is a derisive term used by Frederich Nietzsche to illustrate the kind of morality originating in the slave class, and according to Nietzsche, it values submissiveness, benevolence, humility, and patience. Nietzsche considered these qualities weak and likened Christian virtue to slave morality. Nietzsche contrasted this type of morality with **master morality** seen in the aristocratic, ruling classes, which exemplified pride, moral decisiveness, assertiveness, and affirmation of life.

slippery slope argument: also referred to as the "camel's nose under the tent" and "wedge" arguments; one of the most famous ideas in ethics and politics, it is often used to oppose any change in society involving medicine or restriction of rights. It envisions a continuous slope, where there is a good reason for taking the first step, but where at the bottom of the slope there is a morally repugnant result. Because it will be very difficult to say why, if we take the first step, the same kind of reasons won't also justify going from the first to second steps, it claims that we shouldn't take the first step. If we do, it says, we will soon end up where we didn't want to be at the start. For example, "If **euthanasia** is permitted for competent, consenting adults in cases of terminal illness and hopeless pain, before long, doctors will kill patients for lesser illnesses or for those who have not consented."

social contract: a concept associated with a number of philosophers such as Locke, Hobbes, Hume, Rousseau, and John Rawls, which proposes that humanity's emergence from the savage state of nature to organized, civilized society was accomplished by virtue of a tacit contract among its members and included legal and moral obligations that would ensure the continuation of civilization.

socialism: political system that avoids the totalitarian aspects of communism, but which advocates community rather than private ownership of a society's means of production, and the equitable distribution of benefits regardless of wealth or position.

soft determinism: see **determinism**.

solipsism: the view that because there is no adequate bridge from the subjective mind to the external world, the only thing that exists is one's own consciousness and its contents. Generally, a position adopted as a way of forcing people to think about how much they can really prove about the fundamental assumptions they make each day, for example, that other people have minds like their own and that the world really exists when they go to sleep.

sophism (sophistry): the use of arguments which appear to be strong and persuasive, but which are really fallacious in some way. The word comes from the Sophists of ancient Athens, who taught young aristocrats how to speak well to influence the newly-created democracy there. Socrates hated the **Sophists**, and hence, it is a term of derision.

Sophists: group of transient Greek scholars in the 5th century B. C. who taught argument for the sake of winning to students and who themselves charged money to such students for doing so. Socrates and Plato regarded them as charlatans for their policy of charging a fee for their teachings and because they taught manipulation and persuasion rather than the pursuit of the truth.

sorties: also known as "paradox of the heap;" for example, one drop of water does not make an ocean; adding another drop also won't make an ocean. By this line of reasoning, we can never get an ocean or (if grains of sand) a heap.

soul: the living but immaterial thing that animates one's consciousness, maintains (some think even before birth) an identity throughout life, and (some think) survives beyond death.

sound argument: a valid **deductive argument** whose **conclusion** follows logically from its **premises**, and whose premises are all **true**.

state of nature: the human condition outside of organized society or civilization. Philosophers have disagreed on the description of such as state; some like Hobbes view it as "solitary, poor, nasty, brutish, and short" where each person is in a "war against all;" others like Rousseau see nobility in such a state, positing "noble savages" uncorrupted by private property, schooling, and the artifices of civilized society.

Stoicism, Stoic: school of philosophy founded by Zeno around 300 BC in ancient Greece, it views the world as a divinely organized whole in which all things eventually happen for the best; therefore, the wise and ethical man should be resigned and accept the inevitability of the universe.

straw-man argument: an argument that unfairly interprets the opposing position as so weak and untenable that the power of the opposing position is lost and difficult to support; attacking a position easy to refute rather than the real, complex position of an opponent.

sub specie aeternitatis: Latin, loosely "from the viewpoint of the Eternal;" closely associated with Spinoza.

subjective idealism: see **idealism**.

subjective: a personal point of view, and hence, a possibly odd position; contrasts with **objective**.

subjectivism: the belief that the answer to what is right and wrong is held by each individual's personal beliefs, and that moral decisions are made by consulting one's own conscience.

substance: that which can exist independently of all else; something that is not a quality or predicate but more fundamental; something that has an unchangeable essence, contains properties, and exists independently in reality.

sufficient condition: see **necessary/sufficient condition**.

sufficient reason, principle of: a term associated with Gottfried Leibniz, it is the belief that nothing exists without a reason.

sui generis: Latin, "of its own kind;" unique.

summum bonum: Latin, "the greatest good."

supererogatory actions: over and beyond what is required by morality; deeds of extraordinary goodness that are saint-like.

supervenience: a one-to-one dependence between things at two different levels, such that one cannot have a list of things at one level, A, and not have the corresponding list of things at level B. Used in philosophy of mind to explain how mental states can depend on brain states and yet have different **qualia**.

syllogism: classical style of **deductive argument** that contains two **premise**s and a **conclusion**. For example: all cats are felines, all felines are mammals, therefore all cats are mammals.

syllogism, disjunctive: a **syllogism** where one of the premises is a **disjunctive statement**. For example: to graduate, Mary must choose physics or advanced biology, she did not choose physics, therefore she chose advanced biology.

Syntax: the branch of semiotics that studies grammar and the relation between kinds of words. Contrasts with **semantics**.

synthetic a priori statement: a truth about the natural world that can be known through reason alone, independent of sensory experience.

T

tabula rasa: Latin, "blank slate," it is a term used by some philosophers to describe the mind at birth as a blank slate that has not been inscribed by experience.

tautology: a statement that is necessarily true by virtue of logic, and which says nothing because it provides no information. For example, the statement, "She is either dead or she is alive" is a tautology.

teleological argument: see **design argument**.

teleological ethics: see **consequentialism**.

teleology: the study of the purpose or goal of all things.

telos: Greek, "end, or final purpose."

theism, theist: the belief that a personal God exists who is involved in human affairs. A theist is one who believes in theism.

theodicy: from ancient Greek, "theo" (God) and "dike" (justice); a branch of theology which attempts to defend the existence of an omnipotent and benevolent God, given the existence of evil and suffering in the world. It is an effort to reconcile the existence of evil with the existence of a good God. See also **evil, problem of**.

Thomisim: the philosophy of Thomas Aquinas.

token/type distinction: types are kinds and tokens are examples or instances of types. There are thousands of types of mammals (defined as species), and millions of tokens of these types.

transcendence: the state of being outside ordinary experience or understanding.

transvaluation of values: term originated by Nietzsche, it described the process by which the values attributed to **egoism** (considered evil), and selflessness (considered good) would be reversed, therefore celebrating egoism and condemning selflessness.

truth: a condition in which a statement accurately reflects the world; truth refers to statements, **validity** to arguments. In other words, truth refers to content and validity to good form in arguments. An argument may have good form, like a bottle of wine, but have false premises (bad wine).

Turing machine: a machine designed by Alan Turing in the mid-twentieth century to simulate human **cognition**.

U

ubermensch: German, "overlord, superman;" Nietzsche's term for the superior man who overcomes the mediocrity of ordinary people, who determines for himself what is right and wrong, and who thus places himself above prevailing moral values.

universal: a statement that refers to all the members of the same group and describes that which all the members have in common.

universalizability: the feature of a maxim or principle that makes it capable of being consistently applied to everyone.

unmoved mover, doctrine of: see **prime mover**.

use/mention: see **mention/use**

utilitariansim: ethical theory founded by Jeremy Bentham, James Mill and John Stuart Mill in England in the 19th century that holds that acts are right which produce the greatest amount of happiness for the greatest number of beings affected, and second, that the particular act or rule being considered should produce more such good than any other possible act or rule. **Act utilitarianism** contrasts with **rule utilitarianism**, in that the rule (rather than the rule) is the subject of what produces the greatest good. Utilitarianism is hence a theory about: (1) what is right (good consequences, not motives), (2) maximization (the number of beings affected counts morally), and (3) what creates a good consequence. **Hedonic utilitarianism** holds that good consequences should be understood in terms of tangible pleasures.

utility calculus: the notion held by some **utilitarians**, especially Bentham, that the value of certain rules or acts in bringing about the greatest good for the greatest number can actually be measured in happiness units.

utopia: the term used to refer to an imaginary, ideal world.

V

vagueness: a term describing the imprecision or "fuzziness" of classifying statements, which leads to borderline or "unable to say" cases. For example, baldness is a vague concept: when is a man definitely bald?

valid argument: "invalid" and "false," as well as "true" and "valid" are synonyms in ordinary language but not in philosophy, where only premises or statements are "true" or "false,' and only arguments are "valid" or "invalid." The difficult thing for people to grasp is that validity and truth, as used in philosophy, are two different kinds of relationships: "validity" refers to the logical form of an argument whereas "truth" refers to the relationship of a statement to the objects it describes in the world. So an argument can be valid with false premises and an invalid argument can have all true premises. An invalid argument, then, has some problem with its logical form, such as an ambiguous key term. A valid argument with true premises is called **sound.**

value judgement: an evaluative statement.

veil of ignorance: a concept essential to the theory of **justice** of John Rawls, who asks us to choose in a social contract the structure of a just society without knowing what our sex, race, age, or health will be. When the veil lifts, we will discover who we really are, and as such, John Rawls thinks we will choose to make the worst position as good as possible. It is a theoretical device for forcing us to choose the basic principles of justice through the Golden Rule.

veridical: that which is literally true and presents things as they really are.

verification: the process of ascertaining, either through logical argument or empirical demonstration, the truth of a proposition.

virtue: from Latin, "virtu"; righteous conduct; **virtue** has a Christianized connotation that the ancient Greek **virtues** lacks, whereby a man of virtue does a right thing because it is right or it pleases God (such a sense is not conveyed by the virtues of Ancient Greece).

virtues: as a plural, the term refers to excellences of character that include (as the cardinal virtues) courage, wisdom, self-control, and justice, as well as other admirable traits such as loyalty and compassion. "Virtues" refers to excellences of character identified in ancient Greece, whereas "virtue" is broader and also includes

virtue ethics: the theory of ethics that values **virtue**, or **virtues**, rather than duty or the utilitarian greatest good, as the answer to the question, "What makes an act right?"

W

warranted assertibility: term associated with Dewey whereby knowledge is a process, the end product of which allows us to have such good reason to accept its truth, that it is exempt from criticism.

weltanschauung: German, "world view."

will-to-believe argument: term associated with William James, it describes the act of believing not just because there is evidence to believe, but because it is efficacious to do so.

will-to-power: an idea central to Nietzsche's philosophy: first, as a factual claim, it is the view that all people seek control over each other, and hence, that traditional Christian ethics and religion are just one way of doing so; and it is an ethical claim, where the **ubermensch** transcends the conventional morality of the masses and engages in life-affirming **egoism**.

Z

zeitgeist: German, "the spirit of the times."

Zeno's paradoxes: paradoxes devised by the ancient Greek, Zeno of Elea, to demonstrate the impossibility of motion. See also **paradox**.

Zoroastrianism: a dualistic religion dominant in ancient Persia in the sixth century B. C. that emphasized the struggle between the god of light, and the god of darkness. The meaning of life for each person consists in a struggle between giving allegiance to either, and world history is determined by how many souls support which god. The belief of some Christians in the ongoing battle between Satan and God reflects the continuing appeal of this view.

ISBN 0-07-242096-0

90000